797,885 Books

are available to read at

www.ForgottenBooks.com

Forgotten Books' App
Available for mobile, tablet & eReader

ISBN 978-1-334-97908-8
PIBN 10599967

This book is a reproduction of an important historical work. Forgotten Books uses
state-of-the-art technology to digitally reconstruct the work, preserving the original format
whilst repairing imperfections present in the aged copy. In rare cases, an imperfection in
the original, such as a blemish or missing page, may be replicated in our edition. We do,
however, repair the vast majority of imperfections successfully; any imperfections that
remain are intentionally left to preserve the state of such historical works.

Forgotten Books is a registered trademark of FB &c Ltd.
Copyright © 2017 FB &c Ltd.
FB &c Ltd, Dalton House, 60 Windsor Avenue, London, SW19 2RR.
Company number 08720141. Registered in England and Wales.

For support please visit www.forgottenbooks.com

1 MONTH OF
FREE
READING

at
www.ForgottenBooks.com

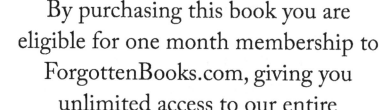

By purchasing this book you are eligible for one month membership to ForgottenBooks.com, giving you unlimited access to our entire collection of over 700,000 titles via our web site and mobile apps.

To claim your free month visit:
www.forgottenbooks.com/free599967

* Offer is valid for 45 days from date of purchase. Terms and conditions apply.

English
Français
Deutsche
Italiano
Español
Português

www.forgottenbooks.com

Mythology Photography **Fiction**
Fishing Christianity **Art** Cooking
Essays Buddhism Freemasonry
Medicine **Biology** Music **Ancient**
Egypt Evolution Carpentry Physics
Dance Geology **Mathematics** Fitness
Shakespeare **Folklore** Yoga Marketing
Confidence Immortality Biographies
Poetry **Psychology** Witchcraft
Electronics Chemistry History **Law**
Accounting **Philosophy** Anthropology
Alchemy Drama Quantum Mechanics
Atheism Sexual Health **Ancient History**
Entrepreneurship Languages Sport
Paleontology Needlework Islam
Metaphysics Investment Archaeology
Parenting Statistics Criminology
Motivational

RAILWAY COEMPLOYMENT

COMPARATIVE LEGISLATION BULLETIN—NO 1—DECEMBER 1905

Wisconsin Free Library Commission
Legislative Reference Department
Madison Wis
1905

CONTENTS

REFERENCES

JUDICIAL DEFINITIONS

HISTORY

LAWS AND JUDICIAL DECISIONS ·

JUDICIAL CRITICISMS

1-14-69

REFERENCES

BEVEN, THOMAS. The law of employers' liability and workmen's compensation. 3d ed. London, 1902.
> Traces the growth of the English law.

CLAY, W. G. Abstract of the law of employers' liability and insurance against accidents in the U. S. and foreign countries. Journal of the Society of comparative legislation, 1897, vol. 2.
> Surveys briefly actual and proposed legislation.

FREUND, ERNST. The police power: public policy and constitutional rights. Chicago, 1904.
> Sec. 633. Absolute liability for personal injuries under other legal systems.

LABATT, C. B. Commentaries on the law of master and servant. vol. 1 and 2, Employer's liability. Rochester, 1904.
> One of the best treatises on the subject. Cases up to spring of 1902.

NEW YORK (STATE)—LABOR STATISTICS, BUREAU OF. Industrial accidents and employers' responsibility for their compensation. (In its Annual report, 1899, vol. 17, p. 555–1162.)
> Gives a general review of the problem of industrial accidents and employers' liability in America and in Europe.

RENO, CONRAD. A treatise on the law of the employers' liability acts. 2nd ed. Indianapolis, 1903.
> Gives the text of the principal American and English acts.

U. S.—INDUSTRIAL COMMISSION. Duties and liabilities of the employer to the employee. (In its Reports, 1900, vol. 5, p. 76–87.)

A brief legal study for the U. S.

—— Court decisions on employers' liability in railroad cases, 1895–1900. (In its Reports, 1901, vol. 17, p. 970–1135.)

—— Compensation for accidents. (In its Reports, 1902, vol. 19, p. 932–39.)

General observations of the Commission.

U. S.—INTERSTATE COMMERCE, COMMITTEE ON (SENATE). Laws of the states and territories concerning employers' liability. Wash. May 23, 1905, p. 108. (Its Regulation of railway rates, Apx. J.)

A convenient compilation giving judicial decisions under the laws of the several states. Can be secured free.

U. S.—LABOR, BUREAU OF. Present status of employers' liability in the U. S. by Stephen D. Fessenden. Bulletin, Nov. 1900, No. 31, p. 1157–1210.

A brief statement of the common and statute law on employers' liability in the U. S.

U. S.—LABOR, DEPARTMENT OF. Workmen's compensation acts of foreign countries by Adna F. Weber. Bulletin, May, 1902, No. 40, p. 549–51.

Gives a summary of the laws of the principal foreign countries in tabular form.

JUDICIAL DEFINITIONS

WHO ARE FELLOW-SERVANTS?

The question who are fellow-servants has been answered in a variety of judicial decisions which present widely conflicting opinions. No other subject known to our law has given occasion for such conflicting rulings. The decisions vary not only for different jurisdictions and for different historical periods but disagree to an extent which cannot be explained on the basis of general principles of law.

Definitions

A general uniformity of opinion is found in the following definitions:

New York. In 1862 the supreme court of New York decided, "Servants are 'fellow-servants' within the rule that the master is not liable for the injuries of the servant received through the negligence of a fellow-servant if they are in the employment of the same master, engaged in the same common enterprise, and are both employed to perform duties and services tending to accomplish the same general purpose, as maintaining and operating a railroad, operating a factory, working a mine, or erecting a building." Wright v. *N. Y. C. R.* Co., 1862, 25 *N. Y.* 562.

Vermont. With respect to railway servants the supreme court of Vermont held that "all who are engaged in accomplishing the ultimate purpose in view —that is, the running of the road—must be regarded as engaged in the same general business, within the meaning of the rule." Hard v. *V*. & C. R. Co., 1860, 32 *V*t. 473.

Illinois. Recently the supreme court of Illinois decided that "the definition of fellow-servants is a question of law; whether a given case falls within that definition is a question of fact." C. & A. R. Co. v. Swan, 1898, 176 Ill. 424.

Wisconsin. Still more recently the supreme court of Wisconsin, in applying the Illinois doctrine, held that "Where there is no dispute as to the respective duties of servants employed by the same master, the question whether they are fellow-servants is for the court." MacCarthy v. Whitcomb, 1901, 110 Wis. 113.

Conflicting opinion

From these definitions it would seem an easy matter to determine what constitutes common employment. The contrary is true.

Field. Justice Field, in C. M. & St. P. Ry. Co. v. Ross, 1884, 112 U. S. 377, says, "This question has caused much conflict of opinion between different courts and often much vacillation of opinion in the same court."

Pollock. Sir Frederick Pollock[1] points out that the term "common employment" is misleading because servants not "about the same kind of work" nor of the "same relative rank" are held to be coemployees.

---

[1] Law of Torts, 7th ed., p. 97.

Classification of Decisions

The decisions may be roughly classified along two general lines: those dealing with inequality of rank in service,—the vice principal rule,[2] and those relating to differences in work,—the departmental rule. However, neither the vice principal nor the departmental rule have uniform application. Pervading both of these rules runs the general doctrine of the assumption of risk.

General Definition

The only approximate definition possible seems to be that,—for any given jurisdiction or any stated time, coemployment is that which the legislature and the courts have defined it to be under the given circumstances.[3]

---

[2] A strict interpretation of the vice principal rule holds only those who stand as substitutes for the master in the performance of non-delegable duties as vice principals.

[3] For a summary of conflicting decisions on railway coemployment see American Digest, Cent. ed., *Master and Servant.*

HISTORY

The doctrine of common employment is of recent origin. The great body of the common law did not embody this principle until near the middle of the 19th century.[1]

COMMON LAW LIABILITY PRIOR TO 1837

It is a general principle of law that the person by whose fault an injury is caused is legally responsible. A further principle is that a person is liable for the acts of his agents acting within the scope of their authority.

In England prior to 1837, the common law principles of employers' liability comprised: 1. The master's responsibility for his own wrongful acts. 2. His liability for the acts of his servants acting within the scope of their employment.

After 1837, it gradually became the rule in England and in the United States to exempt the employer from liability for the injury of a servant resulting from the negligence of a fellow-servant.

---

[1] See,—Pollock, Law of Torts, 7th ed., p. 96. Also Justice Field, U. S. Supreme Court, 112 U. S. 386.

DEVELOPMENT OF THE DOCTRINE

Early cases

1837. The basis of the rule of common employment is found in an English case, Priestley v. Fowler, 3 M. & W. 1.

The doctrine of railway coemployment was first distinctly announced in America.

1841. The first case in this country, Murray v. S. C. Railroad Co., 1 McMulan 385, was decided by the supreme court of South Carolina which affirmed the fellow-servant rule.

1842. The supreme court of Massachusetts affirmed the doctrine in Farwell v. Boston and Worcester Railroad Corporation, 4 Met. 49. This case became the basis for future decisions in the United States and Sir Frederick Pollock[1] points out that it has had weight in influencing English decisions on the question.

1850. The first English case directly deciding the question of railway coemployment was Hutchinson v. York, Newcastle, and Berwick Ry. Co., 5 Exch. R. 343. In this case the Court of Exchequer held that recovery could not be had for a servant of the company, who was on duty on one of its trains and was injured by a collision with another train of the same company, because he was a fellow-servant with those who caused the injury.

Acceptance of the rule

England. United States. From 1837 on a long line of judicial decisions established the coemployment rule in England and the United States.

---

[1] Law of Torts, 7th ed., p. 96.

The Continent. On the Continent the doctrine did not become a permanent part of the law. Tendencies toward the development of the rule were checked by statutes declaratory of employers' liability, and later by the systems of industrial insurance more recently established.

STATUTORY MODIFICATION OF THE DOCTRINE

Statutes Prior to the Industrial Insurance Systems

Germany.[1] Before 1838 the principles of the Roman law held in North Germany and the employer was liable for the wrongful acts of his servants only if he was proven negligent in their selection. In 1838 Prussia enacted a railway law which made railway companies liable for injuries to passengers and others unless they could prove negligence on the part of the injured person or some occurrence beyond their control. In 1871 a similar law was enacted for the entire German Empire.

France. In 1841 it was decided that Art. 1384 of the French Civil Code made the employer liable to servants for injuries due to the negligence of fellow-servants.

Italy. Belgium. Holland. These countries know nothing of a doctrine of common employment.

Norway. In 1854 Norway made railroad companies responsible for the acts of their officials.

Switzerland. Liability for compensation for death or bodily injury to servants was imposed on railways in 1875.

Sweden. In 1886 Sweden made railway companies

---

[1] Compare, Clay, Abstract of the law of employers' liability . . . in Journal of the Society of comparative legislation, 1897.

liable to persons killed or injured in their service excepting in case of accidents due to the disobedience or gross negligence of the person injured.

England. In 1880, was passed the Employers' liability act. Lord Watson in Smith v. Baker, 1891, A. C. 325, said "The main, although not the sole object of the act of 1880, was to place masters who do not, upon the same footing of responsibility with those who do personally superintend their works and workmen, by making them answerable for the negligence of those persons to whom they intrust the duty of superintendence as if it were their own. In effecting that object the legislature has found it expedient in many instances to enact what were acknowledged principles of the common law."

British colonies. In Quebec the doctrine of common employment is unknown. The Canadian provinces and the Australian colonies have passed laws similar to the English act of 1880.

United States. Contemporary statutes for the several states are given under the heading Laws and Judicial Decisions.

Typical Industrial Insurance Systems[1]

Industrial insurance acts providing compensation for injuries due to industrial accidents except those caused by serious or wilful misconduct on the part of the worker are in force in the following countries:

Germany. The compulsory insurance law of 1884, as amended in 1900, provides free medical treatment and a pension of 66 2/3% of wage for either temporary or permanent incapacity and in case of fatal

---

[1] See, Workmen's insurance in Germany and abroad, in Guide to the workmen's insurance of the German Empire, Berlin, 1904.

accidents gives a pension to the family up to 60%
of the annual wage. The annual costs of the system
are assessed on individual employers, according to
wages and risks, by mutual associations of employers
organized by industries, thus securing collective responsibility. The workmen contribute about 8% to
the accident insurance fund. The whole system is
administered by the state.

Austria. The law of 1887 and 1894 differs espec-
ially from the German in having territorial associa-
'ions of employers and employees: the employers pay
90%, the workmen 10% of the costs of accident insurance.

Norway. Compulsory insurance was established in
1894. Employers pay premiums according to wages
and risk. The state pays all expenses of central ad-
ministrative office and one-half of expenses of local
branches; also meets deficits.

England. The act of 1897 applies to accidents in
the more dangerous occupations. Insurance is voluntary, and the costs are paid by the individual employer. Benefits are paid up to 50% of the wages
in case of total disability and in case of death sur-
vivors receive three times the amount of the anuual
wage. Payment is guaranteed by a prior claim upon
amounts due the employer from accident insurance
companies.

Denmark. Established voluntary insurance in
1898. The costs are paid by individual employers,
and compensation may be guaranteed either through
state or private companies.

France. The French system of 1898 is voluntary
except for seamen. The costs are paid by employers
and payment is guaranteed either through state or
private insurance companies.

Italy. The law of 1898 is compulsory. Otherwise it is similar to the French plan.

Switzerland. Compulsory accident insurance was established in 1899; 75% of premiums are paid by employers, 25% by employees. A state subsidy provides about one-fifth of the necessary funds.

LAWS AND JUDICIAL DECISIONS

The United States is the only country in which the doctrine of common employment continues to have great practical significance.

The relation of master and servant has passed from status to contract. The contract relation has been regulated first by common law, second by statutory provisions. The doctrine of common employment has been subject to these two forms of modification and the following pages give the salient points of laws and judicial decisions in the United States.

The fact that many states have deemed it necessary to enact general statutes giving right of action for injuries causing death, without providing for injuries not proving fatal, is explained by reason of the common law right which provided damages in case of injuries, from time immemorial while an action for damages on account of the homicide of a human being could not be maintained prior to Lord Campbell's Act in 1846. (9 and 10, *V*ict. c. 93.)

United States[1]

The decisions of the federal courts on the doctrine of common employment have not been uniformly consistent.

Compare: C. M. & St. P. R. Co. v. Ross, 1884, 112 U. S. 377; and N. E. R. Co. v. Conroy, 1899, 175 U. S. 323.

---

[1] With the exception of citations taken from advance sheets, all cases cited are given from the reports of the court deciding the question.

In 1892 in B. & O. R. Co. v. Baugh, 149 U. S. 368. the supreme court declared that the question as to who are fellow-servants was not a question of local law but rather one of general law, and that in the absence of statutory regulations by the state the federal courts were not required to follow the decisions of the state courts.

In deciding questions arising under the employers' liability acts of the several states, such statutory provisions have generally been accepted as establishing the rule for the federal courts sitting within the state. However, diversity of interpretation has resulted in frequent disagreement between state and federal decisions under the same law.

Alabama. Civ. Code, 1897, c. 43. sec. 1749. Makes employers liable for injury caused by the negligence of any superintendent; or by one in authority; or in obedience to rules or instructions; or by the negligence of any person in charge or control of any railroad signal, engine, switch, car, or train, upon a railway, or of any part of the track.

Liability can not be avoided by contract. A. G. S. R. Co. v. Carroll, 1892, 97 Ala. 126.

Alaska.

In Gibson v. C. P. Nav. Co., 1902, 1 Alaska 407, the vice principal rule was applied.

Arizona. Civ. Code, 1901, sec. 2767. Corporations made liable for injury by fellow servants: previous notice of negligence to be given.

Arkansas. Dig. 1894, c. 130. Railroad companies made liable for acts of vice principals.

Authority must be actually entrusted to vice principal. Hunter v. K. C. & M. Ry. & B. Co., 1898, 29 C. C. A. (U. S.) 206.

California. Civ. Code, 1885, sec. 1970, as amended

by Acts, 1903, c. 220.   Relates to non delegable duties of employer.

In McKune v. C. S. R. Co., 1885, 66 Cal. 302. A train dispatcher was held not a coemployee with a track laborer.

Colorado. Acts, 1901, c. 67. Employers made liable for injuries due to acts of fellow-servants.

Connecticut. Gen. St., 1902, sec. 4702. Default of the vice principal shall be the default of the master.

Delaware. Rev. Code, 1852, ed. 1893, c. 105. A general statute giving right of action for injuries.

A fireman of one train and the brakeman of another are fellow-servants. Wheatley v. P. W. & B. R. Co., 1894, 1 Marv. (Del.) 305.

Florida. Rev. St., 1891, c. 4071, sec. 3. Railroad companies made liable for negligence of fellow-servants. Contracting out, illegal.

Georgia. Civ. Code, 1895, sec. 2323. Liability of railroad companies for injuries to employees.

If an employee is without fault the railroad is liable for the negligence of a coemployee, whether the injury is connected with the running of trains or not. Ga. R. v. Ivey, 1884, 73 Ga. 499.

Idaho. Codes, 1901, Civ. Pro. c. 126. A general statute giving right of action for injuries causing death.

A carpenter employed by a railroad is not a fellow servant of a train dispatcher. Palmer v. U. & N. R. Co., 1887, 2 Id. 290.

Illinois. Ann. St., 1896, c. 70. A general statute giving right of action for injuries causing death.

The duty of a master to warn a servant of danger cannot be delegated to a fellow-servant so as to absolve the master from liability for injury resulting from failure to communicate the warning. (Judgment, 1903, 109 Ill. App. 494, reversed.) Rogers v. C. C. C. & St. L. Ry. Co., 1904, 211 Ill. 126.

Indiana. Ann. St., 1901, sec. 7083. Railroad companies are made liable to employees for injury caused by the negligence of any person to whose order or direction the injured employee was bound to conform; or by obedience to rules; or by the negligence of any person in charge of any signal, telegraph office, switch yard, shop, roundhouse, locomotive engine or train upon a railway; or where such injury was caused by the negligence of any coemployee, engaged in the same common service in any of the several departments, at the time, in that behalf, having authority to direct. Contracting out, illegal. -

No constitutional objection to this act. State v. Darlington, 1899, 153 Ind. 1.

Iowa. Code, 1897' sec. 2071. Gives railway employees a right of action for injuries arising from the negligence of coemployees.

This statute is not unconstitutional, being applicable to all persons or corporations engaged in a peculiar business. McAunich v. M. & M. R. Co., 1866, 20 Ia. 338.

To hold that the injury must have been caused by the actual movement of the cars, engines, or machinery, to come within the protection of the statute would be giving too narrow a construction to the words "in any manner connected with the use and operation of any railway." Akeson v. C. B. & Q. Ry. Co., 1898, 106 Ia. 54.

Kansas. Laws, 1905, c. 341. Makes railroads liable for all injuries to employees in consequence of any negligence of any of their servants. This statute gives to employees of railroads the same right to recover for injuries that a non-employee would have under the common law.

Kentucky. St., 1894, c. 1. A general statute, giving right of action for injuries causing death.

Louisiana. Rev. Civ. Code, ed. 1887, art. 2320. A general provision making employers responsible for damage due to their servants.

Maine. Rev. St., 1903, c. 89. A general statute, right of action for injuries causing death.

Maryland. Code, 1903, art. 67. A general statute giving right of action for injuries causing death.

Art. 23. Provided for a coöperative insurance fund.

Declared unconstitutional, 1904, Court of Common Pleas of Baltimore.

Massachusetts. Rev. Laws, 1902, c. 106. Makes employers liable for injury to employees caused by negligence of superintendents; or by persons in charge or control of any signal, switch, locomotive engine, or train upon a railroad.

Michigan. Comp. Laws, 1897, sec. 6308. Makes railroad companies liable for injuries causing death.

A railroad company is not held to the same accountability toward an employee as toward a passenger. Batterson v. C. & G. T. Ry. Co., 1884, 53 Mich. 125.

But it is due employees to protect them from unnecessary and unusual dangers. Ragon v. T. A. A. & N. M. Ry. Co., 1892, 91 Mich. 379.

Minnesota. Gen. St., 1894, sec. 2701. Makes railroad corporations liable for damages to servants due to the negligence of other servants; does not apply to construction of new road.

Acts, 1895, c. 173. A common law enactment.

Acts, 1895, c. 324, sec. 1. In any action, where damages are awarded for injury by coemployee, the court, upon request of either party, shall direct the jury to name negligent fellow-servant.

The negligence of a fellow-servant constitutes no defense in an action by an employee to recover damages. N. P. R. Co. v. Behling, 1893, 12 C. C. A. (U. S.) 662.

The decision of the supreme court of Minnesota that the fellow-servant law of that state applies to a mining corporation which owns a short line of road to mine its ore is not so clearly beyond the limits of the police power of the state that it must be declared a violation of the constitution of the U. S. Kibbe v. S. Iron Min. Co., 1905, (U. S. C. C. A., Minn.) 136 F. 147.

Mississippi. Const., 1890, art. 7, sec. 193. Makes

railroad companies liable for injuries to employees caused by the negligence of superiors; or by fellow-servants engaged in another department of labor, or on another train of cars, or about a different piece of work. Contracts waiving benefits, void.

Missouri. Rev. St., 1899, sec. 2873. Railroad corporations made liable for damages to servants engaged in the work of operating railroads by reason of the negligence of other employees.

A railroad section hand is within the protection of this act. Overton v. C. R. I. & P. Ry. Co., 1905, (Mo. App.) 85 S. W. 503.

Laws, 1905, sec. 2864. Damages for injuries resulting in death are set at not less than two nor more than ten thousand dollars.

Laws, 1905, sec. 2876a. "Railroads" defined to include street and other railways.

Montana. Acts, 1905, c. 1. Railroad companies are made liable for all damages to employees due to neglect, or mismanagement, or wilful wrong, of other employees in any manner connected with the use and operation of any railroad on or about which they shall be employed. Contracting out illegal. Right of action survives.

Nebraska. Comp. St., 1901, c. 21. Gives general right of action for injuries causing death.

Track repairer, and fireman, not fellow-servants. U. P. Ry. Co. v. Erickson, 1894, 41 Neb. 1.

Foreman of a section crew and an engineer, not fellow-servants. O. & R. V. Ry. Co. v. Krayenbuhl, 1896, 48 Neb. 553.

Nevada. Comp. Laws, 1900, sec. 3983. A general statute, giving right of action for injuries causing death.

New Hampshire. Pub. St., 1891, c. 191. Gives right of action for injuries causing death.

A train dispatcher, not a fellow-servant of a brakeman. Wallace v. B. & M. R., 1904, 72 N. H. 504.

New Jersey. Gen. St., 1895, p. 1188, sec. 10. A general statute, for injuries causing death.

A master cannot claim immunity upon the ground that he exercised due care in selecting mechanics but assumes the burthen of seeing that they actually exercise reasonable care and skill. Collyer v. Pa. R. Co., 1886, 49 N. J. L. 59.

New Mexico. Comp. Laws, 1897, sec. 3216. Railroad companies made liable for injuries to employees due to lack of care in selecting or in overworking servants.

New York. Laws, 1902, c. 600. Imposes liability on employers for injuries to employees caused by the negligence of superintendents or of any person acting as such with the authority or consent of the employer.

The fact that there was a general superintendent who did not take immediate charge of the details of the work, over such foreman, did not relieve the master from liability for the latter's acts. McBride v. N. Y. T. Co., 1905, 92 N. Y. S. 282.

All of the employees of a railway company engaged in operating either of two colliding trains were fellow-servants of a fireman on one of the trains. Rosney v. E. R. Co., 1905, (U. S. C. C. A.) 135 Fed. 311.

North Carolina. Acts, 1897, c. 56. Makes railroad companies liable for acts of fellow-servants. Contracts waiving benefit of law, void.

Held constitutional. Hancock v. N. & W. Ry. Co., 1899, 124 N. C. 222.

North Dakota. Acts, 1903, c. 131. Railroad companies made liable for negligence of coemployees. Contracting out, illegal.

Ohio. Ann. St., 3rd. ed., sec. 3365–22. Persons actually having the power to direct and control, to be held not fellow-servants but superiors; also persons having charge in any separate department.

An engineer on one train is in a separate department

from a brakeman on another train. Railroad Co. v. Margrat, 1894, 51 O. S. R. 130.

Oklahoma.

Decisions of the supreme court of U. S. treated as controlling upon the supreme court of Oklahoma. Cf. Report for 1904, 14 Okla. 422.

Oregon. Acts, 1903, p. 20, sec. 1. Makes railroad companies liable for injuries to employees when caused by any superior; or by any person having the right to direct the services either of the servant injured or of the negligent coemployee; or by any coemployee in another train of cars; or by any one having charge of any switch, signal point, or locomotive; or by any one charged with dispatching trains, or transmitting orders.

Pennsylvania. Digest, 1895, p. 1604, sec. 6. Provides that workmen who are not employees but are lawfully engaged about the premises of a railroad company shall have only such right of action for injuries as if they were employees.

Under this act any one not a passenger, who enters the depot of a railroad company takes the risk upon himself. Gerard, Adm'r, v. Pa. R. Co., 1878, 12 Phil. R. 394.

Porto Rico. Rev. St., 1902. Employers made liable to employees for injuries due to the negligence of superintendents; or to any person in charge of any signal switch, locomotive engine, car, or train in motion.

Rhode Island. Gen. Laws, 1896, c. 233, sec. 14. A general statute giving right of action for injuries causing death.

South Carolina. Const. art. 9, sec. 15. Makes railroad companies liable for injuries to employees due to the negligence of a superior; or of a fellow-servant in another department.

Acts, 1903. No. 48. Benefit from railroad relief

departments not to bar an action for damages for injury caused by the negligence of the company or of its servants.

South Dakota. Civ. Code, 1903, sec. 1449 and 1450. An enactment of the common law.

Tennessee. Code, 1884, part 2, title 3. A general statute giving right of action for injuries causing death.

A conductor of a railway train acting in his official capacity is a vice principal. A. G. S. R. Co. v. Baldwin, 1904, 113 Tenn. 409.

Texas. Acts, 1897, c. 6. Railroad companies made liable for acts of fellow-servants causing injury to any employee while engaged in the work of operating cars, locomotives, or trains.

Hand cars are within the meaning of this section. Long v. C. R. I. & T. Ry. Co., 1900, 94 Tex. 53.

Includes a logging railroad operated by a corporation solely for the purpose of carrying its own lumber. Lodwick L. Co. v. Taylor, 1905, (Tex. Civ. App.) 87 S. W. 358.

Utah. Rev. St., 1898, t. 36. The vice principal rule and the departmental rule applied.

A railroad yardman, not a fellow-servant with a foreman. Armstrong v. O. S. L. & U. N. Ry. Co., 1893, 8 U. 420.

Vermont.

Conflicting decisions. See Sawyer v. R. & B. R. Co., 1855, 27 Vt. 370. Davis v. C. Vt. R. Co., 1882, 55 Vt. 84.

Virginia. Const., 1902, art. 12, sec. 162. Makes railroad companies liable to employees for negligence of servants as follows: employees engaged in the construction, repair, or maintenance of its track; or in any work in or upon a car or engine upon a track; or in the physical operation of a train, car, engine, or switch, or in any service requiring his presence upon the same; or in dispatching trains, or transmitting orders; or for the negligence of superintendents; or of coemployees in another department of labor.

Contracts waiving rights, void. Provisions not restrictive.

See also Acts, 1901-2, c. 322.

Washington. Acts, 1899, c. 35. Liability of railroads for safety appliances.

The negligence of such servants was the negligence of the master in making dangerous the place furnished the plaintiff in which to work. Mullin v. N. P. Ry. Co., 1905, 80 P. 814.

West Virginia. Code, 1899, c. 103. Gives general right of action for injuries causing death.

Trainmen and yardmen are fellow-servants. Beurhing's Adm'r. v. C. & O. Ry. Co., 1892, 37 W. Va. 502.

Wisconsin. Rev. St., 1898, sec. 1816, as amended by Laws, 1903, c. 448. Abrogates the fellow-servant doctrine with respect to railway employees who sustain injuries due to a "risk or hazard peculiar to the operation of railroads." The clause "peculiar to the operation thereof" has been rigidly construed so that the operation of the law is limited to a narrow scope.

Wyoming. Rev. St., 1899, sec. 2522. Contracts of employees waiving right to damages for injuries due to the negligence of other employees are void.

JUDICIAL CRITICISMS

The question of common employment has given rise to a variety of judicial criticism, some severe in denunciation, some commendatory of the doctrine.

Upholding the Rule

Massachusetts.   Chief Justice Shaw of the supreme court of Massachusetts in delivering the opinion in the first important case on the subject of railway coemployment, said "the general rule, resulting from considerations as well of justice as of policy, is, that he who engages in the employment of another for the performance of specific duties and services, for compensation, takes upon himself the natural and ordinary risks and perils incident to the performance of such services, and in legal presumption, the compensation is adjusted accordingly.   And we are not aware of any principle which should except the perils arising from the carelessness and negligence of those who are in the same employment.   These are perils which the servant is as likely to know, and against which he can as effectually guard, as the master. They are perils incident to the service, and which can be as distinctly foreseen and provided for in the rate of compensation as any others.   To say that the master shall be responsible because the damage is caused by his agents, is assuming the very point which remains to be proved." Farwell v. Boston & Worcester R. Corporation, 1842, 4 Met. 49.

South Carolina. In the case, Murray v. S. C. R. Co., 1841, 1 McMullan (S. C.) 385, the first case on railway coemployment to be tried in this country, the court said "No case like the present has been found nor is there any precedent suited to the plaintiff's case . . . It seems to me it is on the part of the several agents a joint undertaking where each one stipulates for the performance of his several part. They are not liable to the company for the conduct of each other, nor is the company liable to one for the misconduct of another and as a general rule I would say that where there was no fault in the owner he would be liable only for wages to his servants."

United States Supreme Court. In the case of the Baltimore & O. R. Co. v. Baugh, 1893, 149 U. S. 368, Justice Brewer of the supreme court of the United States, said "But passing beyond the matter of authorities the question is essentially one of general law. It does not depend upon any statute; it does no spring from any local usage or custom; there is in it no rule of property but it rests upon those considerations of right and justice which have been gathered into the great body of the rules and principles known as the common law. There is no question as to the power of the states to legislate and change the rules of common law in this respect as in others but in the absence of such legislation the question is one determinable only by the principles of that law."

Adverse Criticism

Scotch case. As an illustration of a contrary position taken in an early Scotch case may be cited Dickson v. Ranken, 1852, 14 Sc. Sess. Cas. 2d series 420. In referring to the contention of counsel that the doctrine ought to be adopted on account of its own inherent justice, the court said, "This last recommendation fails with me, because I think that the justice of the thing is exactly in the opposite direction. I have rarely come upon any principle that seems less reconcilable to legal reason. I can conceive some reasonings for exempting the employer from liability altogether, but not one for exempting him only when those who act for him injure one of themselves. It rather seems to me that these are the very persons who have the strongest claim upon him for reparation, because they incur danger on his account, and certainly are not understood, by our law, to come under any engagement to take these risks on themselves."

Ohio. In the case, Little Miami R. Co. v. Stevens, 1851, 20 Ohio 432, the court observed that the "employer would be more likely to be careless of the persons of those in his employ, since his own safety is not endangered by any accident, when he would understand that he was not pecuniarily liable for the careless conduct of his agents."

United States Supreme Court. In holding that a corporation should be held responsible for the acts of a servant exercising control and management, Justice Field said "He is in fact, and should be treated as, the personal representative of the corporation, for whose negligence it is responsible to subordinate servants. This view of his relation to the corporation seems to us a reasonable and just one, and it will insure more care in the selection of such agents, and thus give greater security to the servants engaged under him in an employment requiring the utmost vigilance on their part, and prompt and unhesitating obedience to his orders." C. M. & St. P. Ry. Co. v. Ross, 1884, 112 U. S. 377.

Connecticut. In the case of Ziegler v. Danbury & N. R. Co., 1885, 52 Conn. 543, the court stated, "The defense of ·common employment has little of reason or principle to support it and the tendency in nearly all jurisdictions is to limit rather than enlarge its range. It must be conceded that it cannot rest on reasons drawn from considerations of justice or public policy."

Missouri. The effect of changing economic conditions was dwelt upon by the court in the case, Parker v. Hannibal & J. R. Co., 1891, 109 Mo. 362, as follows: "In the progress of society, and the general substitution of ideal and invisible masters and employers for the actual and visible ones of former times, in the forms of corporations engaged in varied, detached, and wide-spread operations . . . it has been seen and felt that the universal application of the rule (the rule in regard to fellow-service) often resulted in hardship and injustice. Accordingly, the tendency of the more modern authorities appears to be in the direction of such a modification and limitation of the rule as shall eventually devolve upon the employer, under these circumstances, a due and just share of the responsibility for the lives and limbs of the persons in its employ."

CPSIA information can be obtained
at www.ICGtesting.com
Printed in the USA
BVHW071018141218
535632BV00019B/885/P